The Soul of a Woman

The *Soul* of a *Woman*

Philana Allen Crite

Compass Flower Press
Columbia, Missouri

Published by
Compass Flower Press
Columbia, Missouri

Compass
Flower
Press

Library of Congress Control Number: 2024906253
ISBN: 978-1-951960-61-2

Dedication

To Chris with thanks for pushing and shoving me to write down my thoughts and for your unwavering support. You have helped me feel worthy!

Your beauty can only be seen by the wise.
For your beauty is common,
Maybe even grotesquely hidden in the unknown
Or unknowable.
Elephant, whale, manitou.
Beauty in largesse that you overlook.

◉◉◉

When was the last time
you fell in love
with yourself?
The first time?
The feeling I am searching for
is the
falling in love,
in love with,
center of the universe,
just looking at you turns me on
feeling.
I truly haven't fallen in love
with myself.
No wonder I don't see
or understand
the people who have.

◉◉◉

To myself:
  Be love to yourself everyday.
  Make love to yourself in countless ways.
  See your beauty.
  Feel your power.
  Know God within you brings all good
  and created you as good.
  The Goddess of you/me is the central core,
  the Herself that is before the Him that we fail to
  adore.
  Honor Her as you have been taught to honor
  Him.
  Say God she, for that is giving honor to yourself.
  God created them, both male and female.
  Know Her,
  love Her,
  let Her love express through you as you
  the divine female, the Goddess within.
  Love Her body,
  sing Her praise,
  feel Her power,
  be Her joy.
  This is truly what you have been sent here to do.
  Honor that gift and that mission.
  Love yourself everyday.
  Make love to yourself in countless ways.

◎◎◎

I am beautiful, whole, and complete.
I am beauty-filled, love-filled, and peace-filled.
I behold the Divine Being in you.
I love myself enough to keep my word
to myself, to my partner, to my family,
to my community, and above all to God.

◉◉◉

I give myself the gift of self-love daily.
My home, my work, and my play
reflect God's blessings.
I am guided, protected, and prospered daily.

◉◉◉

I care for myself.
I care for myself, everyone, and everything
        as the Creator
does for me.

◉◉◉

Maybe you woke up this morning feeling afraid.
And as the day moved on,
you wondered how you would make it.
As you lay down still feeling unsure.
Stop,
look within,
and listen.
There.
The answer is still speaking to you:
I *am* here,
you are safe,
tomorrow will be better
because I *am* there.

◉◉◉

Today I woke up
afraid and alone.
Sure that I would fail some more
or hurt some more.
And then a quiet voice in my head,
or was it my heart, said,
be still
and know
that you are loved.

◉◉◉

I seek to know and feel all that is life.
If I am all that is,
how is it I can't know it all?
Yet, know it all intimately,
for it is me.

◉◉◉

We are so conditioned to fear and pain; that's what we keep being drawn to and drawing to us. Our unworthiness thoughts and feelings keep some people in our lives disproportionately. Instead of having less of our time and thoughts, they get more.

We actually deny ourselves. And this is unhealthy. For this is not the denial based on achieving an objective and persisting until you succeed. This is self-destructive self-denial where we stand in our own way.

◉◉◉

Any and everything affiliated with love has an effect on us and we want more. I guess that's because we all want more love. Never mind that we fear giving more love to more people.

We all want more of all the things we associate with love. We want more love.

We get more fear. That which we fear the most comes upon us. What we fear is not having enough love.

◉◉◉

Memory often is a gift we fail to see
because we choose to remember
why not or how not.
Yet, when we stop to remember,
we also see how beautiful,
how blessed, and how fortunate it is.
Remember, you can remember
all the beauty
and love
and peace
and know it will come again.

◎◎◎

Use your gift of memory to see
How beautiful it once was
And know that beauty is reborn
With every thought.

◎◎◎

People think they get rid of stress;
But they only dust the furniture!

◎◎◎

Stress does not succumb to,
nor is defeated by drugs and alcohol.
It symbolically feeds with it,
— on it,
— in it.

◎◎◎

Stress got a buzz
(from anti-depressants,
Saint John's wort,
Serotonin,
Neurotransmitters,
Pepcid AC).

◎◎◎

Stress is a passion,
a lustful wench
of questionable origins.
Stress can consume,
or demurely fool you into believing in it.
Funny thing,
stress is really disbelief
— in yourself.

◎◎◎

Surrender your stress!

◎◎◎

Dear Ego:
Be *willing to let it happen.*
I know that you worry and fret
over what's not right,
or where something is.
I feel how scared you get
when you think what you want
won't come or can't happen.
I hear your crying and your raging, doubting voice
when you think I'm not doing it right,
or listening to you,
or making a mistake,
or even having fun when there's work to be done.
I hear, feel, and know your pain
and it hurts me like it hurts you.
Now I ask you to listen to me
because I can hear,
feel, and know another voice.
And this voice brings peace
and joy
and freedom from fear.
This voice,
this still small voice
brings us all that you want.
This beautiful, peace-filled voice
has all the power and substance at it's command,
which it gladly gives to us when we are
willing to let it happen.

⊙⊙⊙

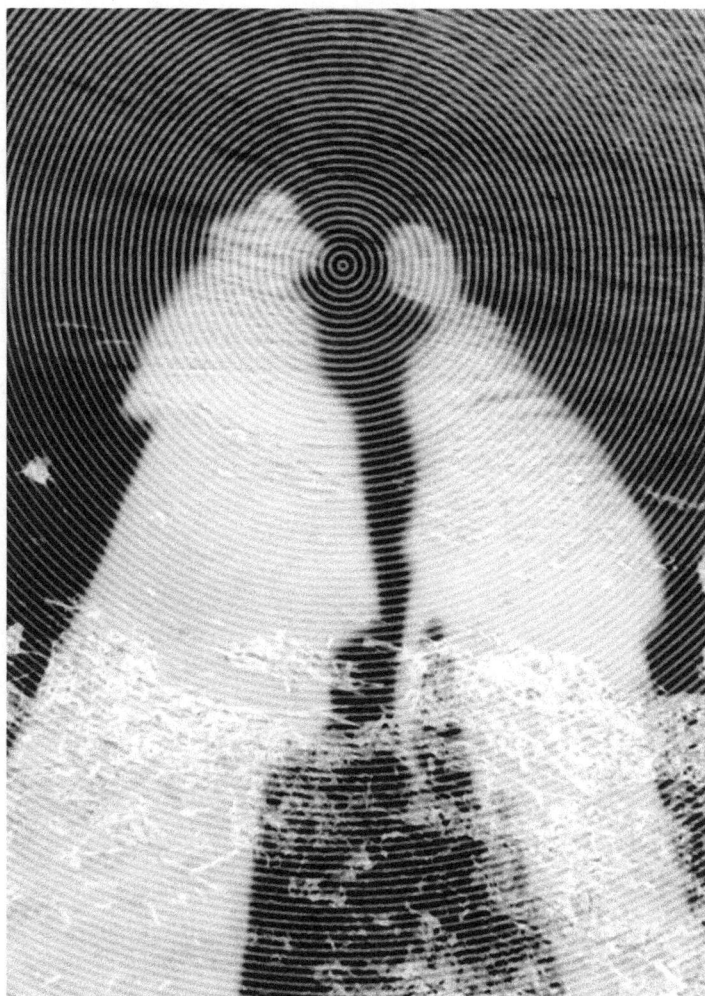

As I looked into a young woman's face,
it seems I saw her mother.
There was a kindness
and a wisdom there
which shown as a gift to her
from her mother,
and a gift for her to the world.
I wonder if faces in us
show the parent we are most like?

◎◎◎

Women are fascinating, alluring, mysterious.
As they walk, the ages of time
pass through each step.
Young and old,
birthing of all life drops from the female.
With each step, seeds of creation
fall from between their legs.
The womb of creation is forever blessing
and sowing
and seeding
and attracting.
All of creation is drawn to the woman,
the female receptacle,
mother of all that is and that will be.
Beauty,
invitation,
hole (whole) of life,
speaker of life,
giver of life.
Woman.
How powerful *I am*.
How wonderous God is in me.

◉◉◉

The Souls of Black Women:
Substance of all matter,
the beginnings of all human life.

Wounded by my abuse,
wounded by our trash,
wounded by too many births.

So full of tears you will not to cry.
So full of pain you will not to feel.
So full of joy you will not to express.
So full of wisdom you will not to share.
So full of love you will not to be.

Heal yourself beautiful one.
Let the Son/Sun shine upon your heartmind
and return to being mother of all life
Birth the life to be in wholeness and trust.
Birth the universe that calls to you from within.

The soul of a Black woman is the heartbeat
of time
and space
and within her eyes lies eternity.

☉☉☉

Thank-You Mom.
Little did I know
how wonderful you are
and how wonder-fully blessed
I am to be your daughter.
As I live life with you
I can daily be renewed to God's love,
for truly God loves us all through you.
Your prayers and your admonitions
bring on good for me
and all your children.
Thank you for being such a giver
and a server of life.

⊙⊙⊙

Grandma:
I feel right now
how wonderful this woman is.
Being still a mother,
nurtured by her mother,
who cares for her mother,
I am truly blessed.
Grandma is a special role;
a double blessing of God,
a Great Grandmother
a precious diamond.

Grandma,
Grandmother,
Grandmommy,
The Mother Dearest to so many.
Her love and wisdom
is as the breath and life of God.
With her coming is great anticipation
and with her leaving such bittersweet sadness.
What a blessing these Grand Women are
and what a joy to be their babies.
I think, for me,
a great joy to anticipate is that
I too, one day,
will have this role to play.

And I have learned
from having the best,
what an honor it is to know
that I will also become
a Grand Mother.

◉◉◉

Dad:
I looked at you today
and remembered how you once played.
Strong and free
and self assured.
Larger than life to all of us.
Your strength, your presence
brought security and safety.
And as you move a little slower,
quietly and sometimes painfully,
I want you to know that I know
in your heart is still
the handsome, strong man who protected us all.
I still see and know your strength
and know that God, through you,
tells me I am safe;
I am loved
and always
am ever watched over.

☉☉☉

Fathers (Oscar the Grouch):
You know fathers don't always get
the ticker tape parades,
the lauds and accolades.
Too often they're working
or fixing
or maybe tired and sleeping.
They're grouchy
and pushing
but always looking out for their own.
In his youth he played
and worked
and it all seemed selfish,
but now I see the old bull still working,
his play now slower
and in different ways.
Yet, still watching over his own,
quietly and stubbornly
showing the way.
keeping it safe and secure
for the little ones to play.

◉◉◉

I think men and women get to be
brothers and sisters
after they have loved as husband and wife
or parent and child.
There is no love like that between loving siblings.
The man/brother loves you for who you are totally.
The woman/sister honors him
as no other ever will—
seeing only the true desires of his heart.
I truly think I feel that no one loves me
quite like my brother.
And truly I look for a man who is like my man/
brother.
Or is that brother/man?

◎⊙◎

My friends appear, it seems,
when I am most in doubt.
And the wonderful thing about them is
that they are also there
when I am in love and having fun.
So, when in doubt,
look for your friends—
remembering they are there for you
in doubt and love.

◉◉◉

Family Spirit

And, yet, she appears as a ghost,
a wisp that comes and goes
from this world to the next.
I'm Special, Wonderful, Beautiful and Deserving.
So how come I keep missing it?

◎◎◎

Divine Substance
Source
Source-ing
Source-er-er
Source-er-ess
Sourcerer- Sourceress
Awaken to your divine
Sourcerer/Sourceress

◉◉◉

I experience God as the greatest of myself.
I experience myself as an extension,
outpicturing of God.
I am an image and reflection of God,
and so are you.
God appears as a woman to me,
in me,
the Divine Presence of me.
Who is God in you?
God is female,
the Divine Feminine
that has remained a mystery.

◎◎◎

I felt a prayer for me today.
Thank you God for prayer partners.
She saw me, for me, through her prayers,
what my fear blinded in me.
Money is the air I breathe.

⊙⊙⊙

The power of a woman
lies in the perceived beauty.
I am always sexy.
I am thoroughly beautiful.
Beauty is inherited.

◉◉◉

How do women see women?
What do we think of and about women?
Why is it this way, and how is it growing or changing?
What do we think women should be or do?

◉◉◉

A beautiful woman
is a prize (is precious).
A beautiful woman
with a good heart
is a treasure.
Outer adornment
is a reflection of
inner richness and beauty.

◎◎◎

How different is a woman's thought and function
if her God(s) is/are female?
If her teachers and ministers and writers are female?

◎◎◎

Do you ever sometimes wonder about feeling?
Who is feeling and how does it come to visit you?
Who is feeling and why does she come like a fury,
like a storm?
This hurricane feeling.
Storms in blowing and pushing her way around,
yet, at her center she is calm.
Yet, like me, pushing, blowing, fury all around.
Yet, my center is at peace.
Oh, to find and stay in that peace.
And the hurricane passes—
more blowing, pushing and fury,
but now, like an afterthought,
a memory,
a might have been
or a want to be
or a should have been
or an almost was.
Hurricane feeling storm,
how is it you came today?
Left tonight—
and is that the sun shining tomorrow?

◉☉◎

God has an infinite source of jobs
and work for me to do.
God is the source
of all employment and money.
God has an infinite supply of money
and work for me to do.
God is the source of my supply of work and money.
God is the source of my supply of security and peace.
Through the Christ of God in me,
I attract and open the doors
of perfect work for abundant pay now.
In the name and through the power
of Christ, Jesus Christ,
I call my perfect work to me and it appears now.
In the name and through the power of Jesus Christ,
my eyes are opened and I see my good now.
In the name and through the power of Jesus Christ,
Christ in me,
I receive all good and abundant money now, today.
My spiritual eyes are opened
and my physical eyes see the place to go,
the path to take and I now arrive at my good.
The perfect work, my place to serve and grow,
my place of abundant prosperity.
God has perfect work,
a job for me to do
and I go to it and do it now.
Because it is of God,
and through the Christ in me,
this work pays me abundantly and brings me joy to *do*.

We want to live and work
where all our frequencies exist harmoniously.
The harmony is natural
and additional creations of Me,
co-creator with God.

◉◉◉

My inner voice, the Holy Spirit in me,
spoke today and said, "go play."
What did that mean?
I wondered in my grown-up mind.
Didn't Spirit know my bills were behind
and there was a job to find?
My Inner Presence spoke today and said,
"Go be with me in the glory
and wonder I am created to be."
Your Inner Presence,
the eternal Life of you,
is calling today and saying,
"Come, soo and be
the wonder you are created to be."

⊙⊙⊙

Protection:
I longed for an Angel the other day,
a sign from God that She cared.
I longed for my Angel to
spread her wings and embrace me,
for I feel alone and unloved.
I longed for an Angel,
a message from God,
and guess what?
My sons loved me
and my checkbook balanced.
Dinner was good
and I saw a beautiful woman in the mirror.
I longed for an Angel today
and ended my day with thanks.
I longed for an Angel today.

☉☉☉

What if God
wanted things, like me and you?
What would God want?
Hmmm?!
Probably the things done
and the creations created in love,
with love,
just as God thought the thought to you.

☉☉☉

God said,
Don't think my thoughts to me,
Build my thoughts as me.

☉☉☉

Remember that all you need you already possess.
Even the brightest of diamonds and gold only
compliment your differing gifts. You came into
this life with all that you need to bring you joy,
beauty and peace.

⊙⊙⊚

What did you want to be when you grew up?
What service did you want to give?
Maybe when you find your inner child,
she soul of you,
you will find your joy.

⊙⊙⊚

Self-discipline is self-study.
Discipline is self-love.

⊙⊙⊚

Do you know the gift you are?
I would guess you don't.
I thought I was doing okay,
And things were moving right along,
But what I realize now is how much
I had given up on myself and of myself.
I see now how much more there was of me to be,
That I was blind to.
Thanks to your loving, divinely guided attention
and affection,
I reawakened to the beauty I am
and the beauty of my world.
Through the many gifts given to you,
you let them pass through you to me
and I am truly blessed.
Thank you for being a gift in my life.

⊙⊙⊙

I'm special, I'm told.
So what do I miss?
I am wonderful, he says,
but I look in dismay.
You're beautiful.
And I ask, who do you say?
I deserve my desires,
and my thought/feeling is *sure, okay*.
What happens between your eye and mine,
your heart and mine,
your mind and mine?
I so want to know her,
the one of which you speak;
I only wish
I could bask
in that love
more often.

◉◉◉

Give your visions back to God.
That is what they are given to you for.

Give your visions back to God
as the physical manifestation
of the ideas of the Mind of God.

Give your dreams, your visions,
your very thoughts
back to the Giver of Gifts,
and the Gift.

⊙⊙⊙

Love persists
and that's a good thing,
because despite
how much I want things to be different,
or want you to change,
or how much disappointment I feel
because we are not together,
I still let love
find it's way through me to you.
Seeing the best
and hoping all good for you.
And I know that
someone feels that same way for me.
Love always fills the gaps
and leaves no one
and nothing empty.
No one void.

◉◉◉

Back to wanting more love.

That may mean: I want more sex, more clothes, jewelry, etcetera, stuff, more affection, less body fat — whatever we have been conditioned to see as associated with love. No wonder we have the difficulties we do.

The subtle conditional behaviors, combined with denial as ego defense mechanisms, keep us forever reaping and sowing — in vain of achieving what we really want.

Everybody wants more love and no body wants to give more love.

We are known by our fruits. How plush, how extravagant, or how barren and sparse.

◎◎◎

Do you invite God into your sex life?
Do you open yourself to God during sex,
before and after sex?
Is God all joy, all love, all peace, all wisdom
a part of your sensuality and your sexuality?
Do you feel/believe that sex is anti-God?
Or that God is anti-sex?
Do you call on God for guidance and help
in expressing your sexual self?

◉◉◉

(What I know is, that) there is something in you
that renews my faith in me.

◉◉◉

Sex is not the issue here.
Sex is good and necessary.
Lust is the imbalance.
Lust is wanting to receive
without giving.
Lust is desiring something
from a lack of consciousness.
Lust is wanting to take something sacred,
or special,
and make it common
or less pure.
Lust is wanting to take from someone,
something sacred and special,
just because you think
you should have it,
or you want to taste it.
Lust is not about sex,
it's about greed
and lack
and feeling love empty.
Lust is filling a bottomless pit.
You will always lust
because you always feel empty.
Knowing truth sets me free,
sets you free from this Hell.

◉◉◉

God is the source of my supply,,
Is in all things.
God is my source and supply of sex.
Only a fool denies their heart.
While the heart must be guided
with the spiritualized intellect
so that there is wisdom,
only a fool denies their heart.
This denial brings
disharmony,
disease,
disfunction,
distress.
There's a beauty in me that I dimly see.
It's shining brilliance
almost too bright to bear.
And what I know for you and me,
is that you have a beauty yet to see.
A shining brilliance
almost too bright
For you to bear,
Yet,
for me,
it feels like
love.

⊙⊙⊙

I also felt the joy
of love in my heat,
As the thought
of my lover crossed my mind.
His kindness and deep abiding love
and respect thrilled me,
and my anticipation grew.
When I turned—
repented, as it were—
from my riotous living
(with all the chaos it brings),
from afar (only for humans,
for there is no distance in God),
God guided me back to
my loved one,
as God guided my love to me.
In my turning I melted,
softened,
surrendered.
For love will have it's way.

Love is powerful,
soft,
gentle,
fierce,
exacting, and all embracing.

Love never lets you
settle for less than your best,
and the pain you feel
in love's presence
is you trying to outpower it.
Yes, in my surrender to love
and my acceptance of it's wisdom,
I understood and happily obeyed.
Today I felt the joy of love as my mind opened.
My soul rejoiced,
and the wedding took place.

◉◉◉

How much we are similar to trees.
How much we gift is free will,
yet we consistently behave as swine before this gift.
How much our beliefs determine who we develop into
And how we appear to the world.
What type of tree are you?
What type of tree am I?
We are known by our fruits.

◉◉◉

How many ways God plays.
As the God people travel from here to there.
All shades and ways.
All kinds of beauty and love.
All outgrowths of God,
Like shoots from some huge tree.
Surprisingly unaware of the other shoots
and even the tree.
Just busy growing,
searching
and moving in the light.
How many ways God plays.

◎◎◎

The ancient ones,
the countless civilizations past
were wise in countless ways.
They knew that there
was more in the heavens
than Earth could think of.
I know that you are protected,
guided and loved.

◎◎◎

The universe is a forgiving place.
A space that ever allows for mistakes.
There's room enough for the itty-bitty ones
that only you can see
and for the giant, giant killers
that seem to threaten me.
The sign says 15 mph.
There are ducks and geese and varmints around.
There are kids and lovers and nature all around.
But away we go, 35 mph plus,
honking our horn at the geese in the way,
missing the tree that fell in the creek
and the sun reflecting off the water.
I came here to relax and slow down
and smell the roses but,
you know, that takes too long
and I only have an hour.
The Universe and, yes, God is a forgiving place —
a space that ever allows for mistakes.

◎◎◎

Let the universe flow through you.
Let life be itself with only your joyful letting,
accepting,
being filled, and
seeing the gold of God in everything.
Relax,
rejoice,
have knowing faith in rebirth.
Open your mouth and speak the truth:
I am special,
I am beautiful,
the universe serves me.
All things are and ever will be.
I did it.
I see you, God.
I bring good news that
God is in you and me as love.

◎◎◎

Park Ponderings I

I watched some people today bring bread to the park to feed the ducks and geese and how the birds did come.

But all of a sudden a woman cried out, "Get away from me, go away," as she threw bread away from her to the birds.

But the birds only knew she brought food and couldn't possibly hear her push them away.

Finally, she ran away, saying "There are too many of them!"

The ducks and geese followed a little and watched the woman leave. The woman still carried the bread with her, unsown, just waiting for another day, when again she would call the birds to her and then cry out, "Get away, there are too many of them!"

Isn't that what cause and effect is? She called it to her by bringing a magnet, an attracting element. Once it was upon her, she wanted it to go away. It could have been people, or problems, or money. She drew it to her and then ran away from it.

◎◉◎

Park Ponderings II

These ducks and geese seem to know that someone will come feed them. They know without an intellect that they must be provided for. These ducks and geese seem to know, from deep within the DNA of them, someone or something will make a way. Surely, I have that same knowing too.

◉◉◉

Park Ponderings III

Do you think these ducks believe that what they need is somewhere else? Do they yearn to leave the pond, because that which they seek for happiness and fulfillment is far away in some distant land or different state? They know, as we can know all you need is at hand.

Open your eyes again and you'll see the riches, the wonder, the prosperity that exists right here, not away from you. And, just remember, someone is coming to where you are. It's their far off land, and begin to say, " How can that be?" Well, just stop and look through new eyes and I know you will find the prize.

◉◉◉

Paradox:
Humble vanity, God's mankind.
Humble vanity, so sure I know.
Until I fall off my bike,
skin my knees
and let Mom kiss them all better.

☉☉☉

I felt the joy of the Lord today.
It came in a different way.
The joy came
as I learned something new,
and as my mind opened out of its darkness,
my soul rejoiced in the dawning.
For my soul had been waiting
on my mind.
And the wholeness of me joyed me.

☉☉☉

All the many gadgets and inventions
of man/woman are reflections of and longings for.
God moves through us to invent and explore,
and at each level where we attain the pinnacle,
invent the weapon to end all weapons,
The machine to do it all,
God moves us somewhere else.
And God keeps expanding just beyond our reach.
It's all good; and
yet, isn't it interesting
how the more movement there is,
It finally ends in silence — a straight line?
Activity leads to peace.

◎◎◎

The shifting breeze,
No wind,
A breath of wind,
Moving the bug sounds to and fro —
How long do the winds blow?
Did East now become West?
There it goes again
Against my left and now my right cheek.
How quickly the winds change.
Shifting breeze,
Breath of breeze,
Moving the bug sounds to and fro —
The winds of change,
My life,
Your life.
Our lives change sometimes like the shifting wind,
No wind,
Breath of wind,
Moving the life sounds to and fro —
A small groan,
A long wail,
A quiet cry
And sometimes the change is a hurricane —
But mostly the change winds are
A shifting wind,
No wind,
Or a breath of wind,
Moving our lives around to and fro —

◉◉◉

New bug sound,
as the chorus changed.
But is that the air conditioner
on the same channel?
Are we just recreating nature
through our machines?
I guess you can't fool mother nature.

◎◎◎

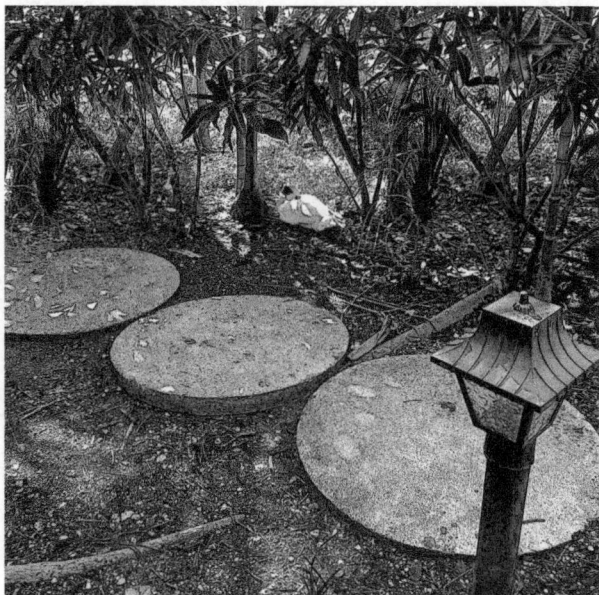

Beliefs
*Our beliefs identify us.
*Our beliefs clothe and house us.
*We are fed according to our beliefs. We feed
ourselves according to our beliefs.
*We feed others our beliefs as well as they eat based
   on what our beliefs bring.

Tree Leaves
*A tree is identified or known by leaves.
*Clothe Tree.
*Sustain a tree by providing food — photosynthesis.
*A tree provides shelter.
*Trees nourish soil when they fall.

My beliefs keep my bedroom messy and confused.
My beliefs keep beauty from expressing in every
   aspect of my personal life.

My beliefs are the limits and boundaries around
   substance
And how it manifests in my life.

There is an all sufficiency, constant abundance of
   substance.

Formless and formed, my beliefs are the stage they
   appear from and show.

⊙⊙⊙

Beauty is in everything, just as God is in everything.

⊙⊙⊙

About the Author

Philana Allen Crite is a semi-retired educator whose interests include science fiction, crystals and music. She is a Cleveland, Ohio native currently living in Columbia, Missouri. She is the mother of two adult sons.